DAVID TAYLOR'S
ANIMALS
IN
BATTLE

DAVID TAYLOR'S
ANIMALS IN BATTLE

Boxtree

INTRODUCTION

M an is a terrible animal, fighting and killing, not just to eat or defend himself, but for a host of other reasons – greed, pride, fanaticism, revenge. One of the things that is unique about the Naked Ape, is his appetite for war – though recently war-like forays by bands of chimps have been recorded.

Man often glorifies and romanticises the idea of battle. Banners and uniforms, brave trumpet calls and glittering weapons – stirring stuff, but fundamentally bitter and tragic. In his wars over the centuries, man the warrior has not fought alone. He has enlisted animals (what sensible creature would ever volunteer?). Animals of many kinds and in large numbers have suffered and died in crusades and conquests, raids and rebellions. Some have played minor, though fascinating roles; while others have altered the course of history.

The Ancient Egyptians, who venerated cats, were defeated in 500 BC by Persian soldiers carrying cats tied to their shields; no Egyptian would risk injuring one of the sacred creatures.

In Ancient Rome geese were used as sentries to guard the city's walls. They would noisily awake sleeping citizens if an enemy approached by night.

In 1796 the generals of the Austrian army, facing defeat by Napoleon, employed a mouse to plan a battle. They dipped its feet in ink and placed it on a map of the battlefield. Where it scuttled, it left a trail of inky footsteps. The general gave orders for their troops to follow the little rodent's route – and lost the battle!

More recently, in 1943, the US Army Air Corps captured 30 million bats with the idea of developing bat bombs. Incendiary devices, each weighing about 30 gm were attached to the bats. It was planned to release the bats over enemy cities where, it was hoped, they would fly into roofs and attics, setting fire to them. Luckily, by the time this idea was perfected in 1945, it was decided not to use them. This decision may have had something to do with the fact that some had already escaped accidentally, burning down an aircraft hangar and an American general's car!

The animals we are going to look at in this book played much more significant parts than cats, geese, mice or bats. Animals ready and waiting for inspection, SIR! ATTENSHUN!

Acknowledgements

The publishers would like to thank the following for permission to reproduce photographs in this book:

Bruce Coleman Limited: pages 7 (M.P. Price); 8 bottom (Carol Hughes); 9, 11 (Jen & Des Bartlett); 12 (Norman Myers); 13 (Jane Burton); 15 (Francisco Erize); 16, 21, 22, 30, 34, 38 (Hans Reinhard); 17 top (Ken Balcomb); 17 bottom (Jeff Foott); 18 (Kim Taylor); 23, 42, 45 (Charles Hennighein); 27 (Fritz Prenzel); 28 (Eric Crichton); 39 (Leonard Lee Rue III); 40 (Gerald Cubitt); 43 (Bruce Coleman).
The Hulton Picture Company: pages 20, 25. Imperial War Museum: pages 8 top, 31, 33, 37, 44. The Mansell Collection Ltd: page 29.

First published in Great Britain in 1989 by Boxtree Limited

Text copyright © 1989 by David Taylor
Artwork copyright © by Boxtree Limited

Front cover illustration and all artwork by David Quinn
Designed by Groom & Pickerill
Edited by Anne Boxendale

Typeset by York House Typographic Ltd

Printed in Italy

For Boxtree Limited 36 Tavistock Street London WC2E 7PB

British Library Cataloguing in Publication Data

Taylor, David, *1934–*
    David Taylor's animals in battle.
    1. Warfare. Role of animals, to 1945
    I. Title
    355.2

    ISBN 1-85283-031-X
    ISBN 1-85283-032-8 pbk

CONTENTS

Abbreviations

mm	millimetre
cm	centimetre
m	metre
km	kilometre
kmh	kilometres per hour
ha	hectare
gm	gram
kg	kilogram

FIGHTING MONSTERS FROM CARTHAGE

*I*magine – it is December in the year 218 BC, and that you, a peasant lad from the hills near the ancient Etruscan city of Saena Julia (modern-day Sienna), have enlisted in the army of Rome. The legion to which you belong is camped in frosty, foggy weather on the banks of the River Trebia about 75 km south of the city we know nowadays as Milan.

It's a hard life – brutal discipline, long marches on a diet of boiled garlic and pickled fish, and bloody skirmishes with hostile tribespeople and Carthaginian patrols. Now, along with your comrades-in-arms of Wolf cohort (a cohort is one-tenth of a legion and comprises 600 men) you wait, trying to draw some warmth from the camp fires . . . waiting for the coming of the dreaded Hannibal, the mighty enemy general from Africa who recently crossed the Alps in a surprise invasion with 70,000 men. Rumours abound as the legionaries sit sharpening sword blades on hard stone and passing round the wine skin.

'This devil from Carthage, this Hannibal, fights not only with men and horses,' mutters your friend Gaius. 'They say he has terrible monsters too.'

'Hah, what nonsense' retorts a soldier crouched on the other side of the fire. 'Women's tales. Now he's in Italy, the Carthaginian dog will face proper Roman steel, not those half-baked conscripts sent against him in Spain, nor those wild Gauls up north!'

You chuckle nervously and wonder what *will* happen when the armies clash.

This elephant charging at you through an African marsh, its ears spread wide, gives an idea of the effect experienced by a defending Roman soldier.

The scouts have brought news that the enemy will arrive tomorrow. They said nothing about monsters though.

During the night you sleep hardly at all under your goatskins. The damp chill penetrates your bones, some of the men sing noisily for hours and always there's the gnawing worry – Hannibal the invincible? Monsters?

Dawn breaks, with the land and the river shrouded in drizzling mist. Officers ride round the camp bellowing orders. There are trumpet calls echoing eerily, the trumpeters invisible in the haze. Standards are raised and men take up their accustomed positions in the battle lines. The smells of wood fires, horse dung, sweat, leather, garlic and wet grass hang in the dank air.

'The enemy is drawn up 500 paces away,' says the man who stands to your right, pointing the way with one of his throwing spears. 'Curse this fog, they'll be upon us before we can see them.'

An hour passes. Excitement and fear make you forget the cold. The Roman legion is by now in perfect order; the men,

A working Indian elephant effortlessly carries a tree trunk up a riverbank in Nepal.

clad in metal helmets and leather cuirasses have formed three lines. They are armed with large shields and short thrusting swords, with the addition of throwing spears in the front two lines and long spears in the third line. And they are ready for anything.

A distant trumpet blares. A chorus of voices gets steadily louder somewhere in the mist in front of you. More noises – of feet tramping, metal clanking, animals snorting – can be heard. The enemy approaches. You see shadows in the gloom, darkening, enlarging.

'Steady, lads!' your officer barks. 'Throw true and throw hard when I give the word!'

Spears jut like a hedge of iron thorns. Surely your line of armed and bristling men is impregnable. Then it happens – through the smoking, vapour-laden air, 20 paces in front of you, looms a veritable demon of enormous size. You blanch. It's true! THEY DO HAVE MONSTERS!

Above: *The pulling strength of the elephant is put to good use.*

Below: *'I'll just sip a quick gallon or two.' Elephants love taking a dip.*

Flesh and blood, it moves rapidly towards you. It is horrible to behold: as big as a house, coated in armour and glistening spikes, the head grotesquely sprouting a writhing snake like that of the fabled Gorgon, and with legs the size of the trunks of oak trees.

The demon bears down on the front rank, and in a babble of cries and the thud of weapons falling to the ground, the cohort (ye gods!) is split. Men tumble as the demon smashes through, followed closely by yelling Carthaginian foot soldiers slashing left and right with sword and spear. Though you don't realise it, you and your comrades have seen your first *elephant*.

Within minutes several dozen of these biggest of all land animals have routed the famous legions of Rome, and Hanni-

bal of Carthage can celebrate a great victory – he and his army, and his elephants, have won the battle of Trebia.

Elephants had been used in battle before Hannibal of Carthage employed them so brilliantly, but not by the Romans. In fact probably few Roman soldiers had even seen one, let alone knew how to fight it. At Trebia these gigantic animals, carrying armour to protect the few vulnerable parts of their bodies from spears and lances, broke through the formations of infantry (foot soldiers) like modern tanks. The cavalry (horse-mounted soldiers) to the rear was in a shambles for horses have an instinctive dislike of elephants. It was

'Don't you dare try anything on while my mum's around!' A baby African elephant sticks close to its mother's side. He can look forward to a long life – up to 70 years!

only later when the Romans captured some elephants and learned for themselves how to train them for warfare that they understood how to combat them. In future battles foot soldiers would be instructed to part their ranks when the elephants charged at them, and then, as the mighty beasts rushed through, use their swords to slash at the creatures' Achilles tendons (the gristly tendons at the backs of their ankles) in order to disable them.

Hannibal's march

Hannibal's famous journey across the Alps with a large army and 37 elephants began in spring 218 BC on the Spanish coast south of Alicante in the Costa Blanca. As a life-long enemy of the Roman Empire, he hoped to conquer Italy for the rival empire of Carthage. He moved up the coast and into France until he reached the River Rhone. To fool the Romans into thinking that he wasn't interested in crossing over the Alps into Italy, he then turned north up the left hand bank of the Rhone. Once the Romans had been fooled into thinking he was on a harmless expedition against the Gauls, he quickly turned eastwards again, crossed the Rhone by rafts, and marched for the Alps. Amazingly, he crossed the high mountains, probably via the pass of Mont Genevre, without losing a single elephant to disease or injury. He descended into Italy and began a series of victorious battles by defeating the tribe that inhabited the city of Turin. The terrorising effect of the elephants on men who had never seen or heard of such creatures, together with their immense bulk and unstoppable power, gave Hannibal's army a formidable advantage.

In April 1988, I retraced the route of Hannibal's epic march in the company of Ian Botham, the English cricketer, and three Indian elephants from an Italian

circus, and we successfully raised a large amount of money for the Leukaemia Research Fund in the process. Our elephants fared as well as Hannibal's though we only asked them to walk a few miles each day at a speed they chose. The rest of the time they spent travelling by circus wagon to the next stop, where they were turned out into a field, to wait for us to catch up with them. My job was to act as Jumbo GP and walk with them to see that they stayed in tiptop condition. The elephants arrived in Turin fitter than me!

There used to be more than 350 different kinds of elephant on earth, but almost all became extinct long before Hannibal defeated the Roman army at Trebia. By then there were only the two species we know today – the *African* and the *Indian* (also known as the Asiatic) elephant. We don't know for sure which kind of elephant Hannibal used on his expedition. Some historians say African – Hannibal came from Carthage which was an ancient town in North Africa, in what today is Tunisia. Indeed, there are ancient Carthaginian coins of Hannibal's time which are engraved with unmistakable African elephants. One way you can recognise an African elephant is by its much larger ears. But there are other experts who think Indian elephants were used, as they are easier to train. There are Italian coins issued about the time Hannibal marched into Italy that bear the images of Indian elephants. This is a mystery that will probably never be solved.

The most formidable of all land animals. An elephant herd on the march in Namibia.

Fearless and formidable

Elephants are naturally fearless and formidable animals. Weighing up to 6 tonnes, eating 200-300 kg of food a day, and with thick, but sensitive skins, they have no natural enemies, although tigers may infrequently take them on. They are short-sighted, but possess marvellous hearing and a sharp sense of smell.

An ancient forerunner of the armoured car: war elephants were also used by Indian Rajahs.

*Seest thou not
How thy Lord dealt
With the Companions
Of the Elephant.
Did He not make
Their treacherous plan
Go astray?
And He sent against them
Flights of birds
Striking them with stones
Of baked clay.*

This verse or Sura is called 'The Elephant'. It comes from the Holy Koran of Islam and refers to an historical event that happened about the year AD 570 when Mecca was invaded by the Christian Abraha of Abyssinia with his war elephants. The birds which flung stones at the invaders were thought to have caused an epidemic, characterised by sores and boils, that ravaged the Christians; this may be a reference to an outbreak of plague.

THE SUBMARINE SOLDIER

*I*magine. You are Lieutenant Yuri Zhukov of the Special Services Underwater Unit, Red Banner fleet, Russian Navy. The mission, like all others, is TOP SECRET. A new design of American frigate with a revolutionary propulsion system has been put into service according to intelligence reports received from the Soviet Embassy in Washington. The ship is faster and quieter by far than anything that the USSR possesses. What the spies *haven't* been able to discover, however, is what the new system looks like when fitted to a vessel. In place of a propeller there exists – what? Only one way to find out – go and take a look underwater.

And now one of the new frigates is on a visit to Portsmouth in southern England. The harbour is heavily guarded on land, and the vessel is surrounded by patrol boats that circle her protectively night and day. Your commander has given you your orders: 'Go in by silent nuclear submarine to a point about two miles off Gosport beach. Ride on an underwater scooter to the harbour mouth with an incoming tide. After that Yuri, you must do it the hard way. Leave the scooter and swim in, 4 m deep.'

The time is midnight on a moonless night. You are clad in an all-black wet suit with your face blackened. Strapped to your back are two air tanks painted black, part of a sophisticated breathing system that will not release tell-tale air bubbles to the surface once you are underwater. You will navigate by luminous instruments attached to your wrist. Shutting off the scooter's motor, you leave it lying as planned beneath an old iron buoy. With a powerful kick of your flippers, you glide into the cold darkness. Soon you see glimpses of light through the murky depths of the water, coming down from the harbour buildings and the moored ships. The water becomes dark-grey instead of black. You can pick out a ship's keel in the deep gloom. Checking your

Three 'Flippers' show their teeth. The teeth of bottle-nosed dolphins are not for chewing but rather grabbing hold of fish.

plastic map with a tiny water-proof pencil-torch, you change course. Another 200 m maybe. There is the low chugging of a patrol boat overhead. You hang in the water till it passes. There – a black wall emerges out of the half-darkness; it is the frigate's hull. You look around you, turning in the water and listening intently – no sign of frogmen guarding the ship. You feel elated – no-one knows you are here, no-one would expect you. You are as black and silent as the deep water itself, invisible to their searchlights, undetected by their sonar. You move on, feeling for the mini-camera attached to your belt.

Suddenly you sense something near you and jerk your head to your right. A shape, a shadow is cutting through the water straight towards you! It travels too fast, too smoothly for a man. A shark? No – not in these waters. A second later the bayonet strapped to the head of a *dolphin* slams into your chest. With one last gasp you sink helplessly to the bottom, all consciousness draining away. The frigate's secret remains a secret. The dolphin sentry swims off with a leisurely upward

flick of his tail, for *his* sonar tells him that you were alone. For him the threat is over and his task accomplished.

Although the above story is horrific and may sound bit far-fetched, Atlantic bottle-nosed dolphins (the 'Flipper' you see on TV and in marinelands) really have been trained to do this sort of deadly guard duty, and have seen active service with the US armed forces for many years. In Vietnam, for example, their function was to guard harbours and ships at anchor against enemy frogmen; in Nicaragua they planted mines; and in the Arabian Gulf they searched for them.

For over 25 years the US Navy has maintained an Undersea Warfare Department to study the potential of the fighting dolphin. This has, incidentally, made many valuable scientific discoveries which have helped us to understand better this magical mammal and to unravel some of its secrets. Spin-off from the military dolphin programme has been of great benefit to research into human deafness and blindness, and into serious health threats that face deep-sea divers.

Living torpedo

Dolphins are highly-qualified recruits for modern sea warfare, I'm sad to say. They are intelligent, nimble, fast-moving creatures, with great strength and many inbuilt mechanisms for mastering the undersea world. They can be trained to fill various roles, particularly that of silent-running and elusive living torpedoes!

Though dolphins have large, efficient eyes which see well both above and underwater, it is their *sonar* ability which enables them to function just as well in pitch darkness, at night or far beneath the waves. The dolphin sends out a beam of sound 'blips' that bounce off distant objects, producing an echo that returns to the animal and which is analysed by it. These echoes are received, oddly, by the tip of the chin (*beak*) and the 'armpits' (where the flippers join the chest wall), and they are channelled by sound-conducting pathways to the well-developed internal ears. With its sonar system, a dolphin can *hear* the scene around it. The echoes tell the dolphin where, and exactly what, a far-away object is, and what it is doing. Dolphins can distinguish for example between a herring, a small shark and a mackerel. They can even tell the difference between different kinds of metal.

Although much of the US Navy's work with dolphins is still classified as secret, it seems probable that they possess animals which can identify particular types of sub-

Swimming at speed, dolphins often leap exuberantly out of the water. Two Pacific bottle-nosed dolphins enjoy the sunshine on their backs.

marines and other craft. Dolphins have been trained to carry magnetic limpet mines and stick them onto the hulls of enemy vessels. Their speed and manoeuvrability pose immense problems for defending frogmen and harbour security systems. So far nobody has developed the idea of having trained killer whales to act as watch dogs to combat dolphin raiders! Dolphins cut through the water at speeds of 40 kmh or more, their special skin eliminating drag and turbulence; and they can kill with a powerful blow of their

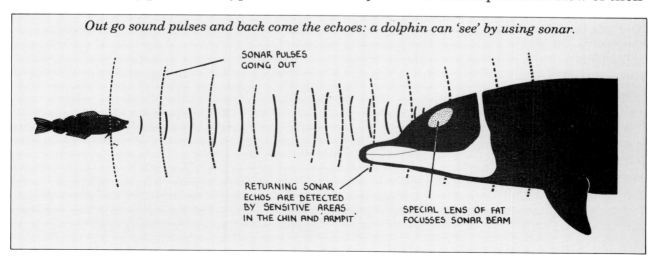

Out go sound pulses and back come the echoes: a dolphin can 'see' by using sonar.

SONAR PULSES
GOING OUT

RETURNING SONAR
ECHOS ARE DETECTED
BY SENSITIVE AREAS
IN THE CHIN AND 'ARMPIT'

SPECIAL LENS OF FAT
FOCUSSES SONAR BEAM

The friendly and inquisitive bottle-nosed dolphin. What a pity it should sometimes be trained for military purposes.

closed jaws. They frequently kill marauding sharks that menace baby dolphins by punching them in the under-belly in this way. To avoid accidents, friendly Navy frogmen identify themselves to their sentry dolphins by wearing electronic 'bleepers' on their belts. These emit a sound signal that the dolphins have been trained to recognise. Nevertheless the US Navy has admitted that things have occasionally gone wrong and that the dolphins have mistakenly attacked and killed their own men.

Dolphins, and even sealions and small whales, have been trained in America to locate mines and missiles underwater. Once found, the animal will swim down to the object carrying a device in its mouth which is attached to the object by means of a magnet or a spring-loaded clamp. A small compressed gas cylinder then automatically inflates a balloon which rises to the surface on a length of cable, so marking the object's position. Sometimes the balloons are big enough to lift the mine or missile up to waiting scientists.

A special relationship

Dolphins have many qualities that make them valued members of the Navy. They can dive deep and stay underwater for long periods of time. They can work easily without light in the dark depths of the sea. And once their job is done, they can rise rapidly again to the water's surface without getting 'bends'; a dangerous condition caused by bubbles of nitrogen gas appearing in the blood. Of course the key to it all is that dolphins love to work with or for human beings. Long ago the Romans called in wild dolphins each year to help them herd fish into traps on the French coast near Marseille, rewarding them afterwards, it is said, with 'bread soaked in wine'; and we regularly hear of drowning people being saved by dolphins which have supported them and pushed them towards the shore.

What a tragedy that such wonderful creatures should ever have to be involved in man's dirty business of war and destruction.

Above: *A streamlined fast-moving species of the deep ocean, the Pacific white-sided dolphin.*

Below: *Making friends. This air-breathing mammal is quite happy to come out of the water and be stroked.*

*I*magine. It is the end of November in the year 1870. You, Henriette Crapaud, sit in a cold, dark room near the cathedral of Nôtre Dame in Paris, France, wondering whether you can ever bring yourself to eat the piece of roasted rat that Mme Blanc, the concierge, has prepared for you. Rats, weeds, once even a dog – this is what hunger has brought you to. But you are not alone – all the citizens of Paris are starving, and disease is rife. There seems to be no end in sight. With Prussian armies besieging the capital and the air trembling with the boom of shell fire, there is despair everywhere. The Emperor Napoleon III has been captured and the statesman Gambetta has escaped from Paris by hot air balloon to try to raise an army to relieve the city, but like most folk you reckon it can only finish in a humiliating surrender to the Germans.

You are an assistant to the Parisian inventor and engineer M. Prudent Dagron, who nowadays earns barely a *sou* and cannot afford to pay your wages. But he's a good man, and maybe when the war is over he will take you to London to see some of the new English machines he talks about so much.

Unable to face the food, you put on your bonnet, coat and muffler, leave the house,

The sheer beauty of fantail pigeons rising into the air against a winter sun.

The secret agent successfully carries the microfilm through the enemy lines.

and walk across the Pont Sully. You pass a group of grimy soldiers huddled around a brazier, eating blackened onions. After five minutes you reach M. Dagron's workshop. As usual the inventor is seated at a bench littered with tools, glistening brass instruments and bottles of chemicals. A tall, bewhiskered man in a faded, blue, military uniform is standing by the window.

'Bonjour, Monsieur,' you say as you enter.

'Bonjour, Henriette,' replies Dagron. 'Oh, this is Captain de la Grange of the Imperial Artillery.' You shake hands with the stranger then go to your bench to begin your work.

'Henriette, Captain de la Grange has come to us with a problem – and I think we can help.'

'What is that, Monsieur?'

'The garrison here in Paris urgently needs to send maps of the disposition of our troops to the Commander-in-Chief with the French forces south of Versailles.'

You frown, puzzled. 'But how can we help, Monsieur?'

'The maps, my dear girl, are numerous and bulky – they must be photographed.'

M. Dagron has been a keen photographer for years – his workshop reeks of burnt magnesium flare powder. But you are still puzzled. 'But the photographs will also be big, Monsieur – what will you do with them?'

Dagron smiles. 'The Englishman, Henriette, the Englishman. He gave me the idea. Way back in 1853 when I first went to London, I met an Englishman, John Dancer, a maker of optical instruments who had recently reduced a full page of *The Times* newspaper to a dot barely 1.6 mm across! A sort of reduction photography! I have the lenses and the camera. I'll do the same.'

'M. Dagron here says he can shrink our maps to pinheads,' interrupts the Captain. 'A great idea!'

A pigeon, serving with the Army Pigeon Service in Africa in 1945 carries a special container on its back.

'And how will you send the photographed dots through the German lines, Monsieur?'

'Simple, Henriette, simple,' replies Dagron with a soft chuckle. 'Over their heads! By *pigeon*, my dear girl. A pigeon shall be our secret courier!'

Microdot carriers

It really happened that way. Prudent Dagron *did* photograph and reduce to the size of dots many pages of military information. He is recognised as the inventor of the 'microdot' which is still employed by spies and secret agents. The dots were printed onto photographic emulsion which was then wound into a thin tube and fastened to a pigeon's tail feathers. One pigeon could carry 18 emulsion films

and each film could contain up to 3,000 messages. The pigeons returned to their home lofts in the countryside outside Paris flying over the city's barricades. The film was recovered from the tube, and the dots were then magnified and read using a 'magic lantern' projector. And so the pigeon was enlisted into the French army's Intelligence Service.

Pigeons were first domesticated in Ancient Egypt around 3,000 BC and had been used as messengers long before M. Dagron thought of his microdots. The Sultan of Baghdad set up a pigeon-post system in the year 1150 AD. It lasted for 108 years until Baghdad fell to the Mongol invaders. And in France during the 1848 Revolution it was common for short messages to be sent on pieces of paper attached to pigeons for publication in French and Belgian newspapers.

During the twentieth-century the pigeon has played an important role in espionage. In the early 1900s, Herr Neubronner, a German, developed a miniature automatic camera weighing a mere 70 gm which could be carried aloft by pigeons to be used for spying and military reconnaissance. During the First World War (1914-18) the French Army employed thousands of pigeons to carry vital messages, and one bird which died after a successful mission flying through intense artillery fire at Verdun was actually awarded a posthumous Legion d'Honneur, the Republic's highest decoration. In the Second World War (1939-45) British planes dropped boxes of homing pigeons by parachute into German-occupied Europe to be used by the resistance fighters to fly messages to London.

The choice of pigeons to do such important work was quite natural. A common, domesticated species, the bird can reach speeds of 96 kmh and can cover distances of perhaps, as much as 12,800 km. An enemy wanting to intercept pigeon-borne letters might perhaps think of using birds of prey like falcons as 'fighters'. But first he would have the very difficult task of identifying pigeons 'on active service'.

Many experts, however, consider that no peregrine falcon in level flight could catch a fast racing pigeon, although these hawks can *dive* at 131 kmh.

A natural counter-spy, the peregrine falcon could be used to intercept message-carrying pigeons.

Amazing navigation

The master trick that the pigeon shares with many other birds, is its ability to find its way through the skies. Scientists still do not fully understand the pigeon's amazing ability to navigate with precision. They can do it by day or by night and with the sun, moon and stars behind cloud. It appears that they use a complicated system involving taking sitings of the sun or stars, perhaps by means of an organ in their eye called a pecten, much in the same way as a sailor uses a sextant. Some scientists believe the pecten also functions as a magnetic compass. Quantities of magnetic iron, which form a simple

Right lads, see you at the finishing line. Racing pigeons in their home loft.

compass, have been found in the skull of the pigeon, and it is known that pigeons can get lost if flying over places where large underground iron deposits distort the earth's normal magnetic field. Perhaps pigeons plot their courses by reference to our planet's invisible lines of magnetic force. This would account for the fact that pigeons can find their way home even on the cloudiest night when no stars are visible in the skies.

As well as the pecten and the compass, pigeons also possess an in-built biological 'clock' together with the ability to read the star map of the heavens and, when nearer home, to recognise familiar landmarks. Just as for a human navigator, a clock and a map will help the pigeon to judge how far it has travelled, and when it is time to change course.

Of all the military uses of animals, the one of which I most approve is the 'spy in the sky' role of the pigeon. These familiar birds of London's Trafalgar Square and Manhattan's concrete jungle must have saved many human lives.

Right: The natural navigator. Birds like this pigeon possess an in-built clock, compass, star-map and possible sextant.

Below: Ultra-fast flash photography catches a pigeon about to land on its perch.

ANIMALS THAT CHANGED HISTORY

*I*magine. It is June in the Year of Our Lord 1099 in the land we now call Turkey, not far from the important city of Antioch. For you, Count Roland of Moze, these are stirring times. The First Crusade began two years ago when, blessed by the Pope and inspired by the fiery, wandering preacher, Peter the Hermit, 300,000 Christians, mainly Normans, knights and nobles, peasants and priests, merchants and mercenaries, set out from Europe with the Cross as their standard to recover the Holy City, Jerusalem, from the grip of the Seljuks, an Islamic Turkish tribe. You recall well the fierce fighting as you passed through the Byzantine kingdoms of Hungary and Bulgaria, the gathering of the hosts at Constantinople in Spring 1097 and the great cathedral of Santa Sophia packed with armoured men at High Mass. You remember too the first clashes with the Seljuks who rode into battle under the green banner of the Prophet Mohammed. And you will never forget the heat, the searing heat, of Asia Minor.

Now, in a column 5 km long, archers marching in front, plumed knights prancing behind, you ride on your faithful black stallion. The arid, grey land, broken only by low hillocks of crumbling rock, stretches in all directions to meet a grey sky on an imperceptible horizon. It is hot and humid. No wind, but many flies. Your chain-mail, helmet, leather under-jerkin, sword, axe and dagger weigh heavy. The stallion gleams with sweat where it is not covered in leather and mail. Oh, to fight again on the green swards of England or in the cool valleys of the Rhine! This ceaseless, sticky heat punishes more than any Mohammedan scimitar.

Still, once in the Holy Land, there will be riches to be had. Maybe you will be given a small kingdom for yourself by a grateful Pope. Yes, soon you will be in Jerusalem; there can be no doubt, for only a week ago the true Holy Lance that pierced the side of Our Saviour when He was on the cross was discovered – a sign of heaven's benediction indeed.

Your thoughts are rudely interrupted by a 'thwack' sound. An archer walking immediately in front of your horse falls to the ground, an arrow sprouting from his neck. Uproar breaks out at once. There is shouting and the metallic hiss of swords being unsheathed. Archers unshoulder their bows, horses snort and rear. Over to your right, 50 paces off, you see a horseman in turban and flowing robe disappearing behind a hillock. Mohammedans!

Horses as well as men suffered at the Battle of Waterloo.

Two of your armoured knights are already riding after him. They quickly return. 'Gone, my Lord,' one calls. No wonder, you think. These heathen bowmen on their light and agile horses carry no armour, and have often little more than rags to cover them. Norman knights clank around in iron on lumbering heavy steeds. By Our Lady, if only these Mohammedans would fight like we do in Europe. Steel against steel. But no! They prefer to harry us, pick us off piecemeal, all by dint of speed, surprise and flexibility. It's just not Christian!

So it was that crusader and Moslem *horses* met in battle, with large numbers of animals dying as a result, though in some encounters such as that at Jaffa in 1191, only two crusaders lost their lives. In all the most crucial battles and expeditions throughout history, the horse was present and played a leading role – in the conquests of Alexander the Great, at the Battle of Hastings in 1066, in the struggles between Royalists and Roundheads in the English Civil War, at the Battle of Waterloo in 1815, and in the American Civil War (1861-65), man and horse fought and died together. The names of individual battle horses have come down to us through the pages of our history books – there is *Bucephalus* who belonged to Alexander the Great, the only person who could mount him; *Incitatus*, the Roman Emperor Caligula's stallion that was said to have drunk wine out of a golden bucket; *White Surrey*, the favourite horse of King Richard III; and *Copenhagen*, the Duke of Wellington's faithful charger.

Ancestors of the horse

How did the horse develop to become man's most important domesticated animal? The story begins about 55 million years ago. Then the continents of Europe and North America were joined together in one land-mass. Here a little dog-like animal moved through the forests, browsing on low shrubs. This was *Hyracotherium*, ancestor of the horses and also of the rhinoceroses and tapirs. It was descended itself from forebears which had possessed the basic five toes per foot, and it had already lost two outer toes on its hind feet and one inner toe on its fore feet. The remaining toes looked dog-like, with pads; but as yet there was no sign of hooves. It had a short muzzle and a long tail held curved like a cat's.

As the ages passed, the descendants of Hyracotherium split off into numerous branches of the family tree. The rhinos and tapirs went their way and the horses went theirs. In the equine branch, many developments took place over thousands, even millions of years. Gradually more toes were discarded till finally a single, highly modified toe remained on each foot. The animal grew larger, developed teeth that were ideal for cropping and grinding grass, and acquired large, efficient eyes.

By about one million years ago, all the surviving equine descendants of Hyracotherium had settled into four main groups: the *horses*, the *asses*, the *half-*

An unlikely animal for the Grand National! Hyracotherium, the early ancestor of horses and ponies.

asses and the *zebras*. They were distributed in fairly specific areas of Africa, Europe and the Middle East, with almost no overlapping of the various groups. The zebras were to be found only in the south of Africa and the half-asses (ancestors of the *onager, kulan, kiang and dziggetai*, and of the *hemione* which became extinct about 100 years ago) were all from Asia. The asses, from which *donkeys* were developed, were purely from the north of Africa, and the horses (including *ponies*, which are simply horses under 14.2 hands high) were inhabitants of Europe and western Asia.

By the Ice Age, scientists can identify four major types of horse or pony existing in the world, and with the disappearance of all horses in the Americas by about 6,000 BC (why, we do not know), they were confined to Europe and western Asia. From those four types the cavalry horses of history as well as our modern horse and pony breeds are all descended.

Domestication of the horse began around 3,000 BC, almost certainly in eastern Europe and the steppes of western Asia (at about the same time the Sumerians started domesticating onagers in what is now Iraq). From these areas the domestic equine spread outwards after 2,000 BC, with the first animals being

> *With a host of furious fancies*
> *Whereof I am commander,*
> *With a burning spear, and a horse of air,*
> *To the wilderness I wander.*
>
> Anon 17th Century

Our ancestors looked at the horse with its strength and mobility and slowly began to realise how this fine beast could change things – not least in the art of warfare. At first the fighting men of Europe were foot soldiers; early Greek and Roman armies were composed almost solely of infantry, with sometimes just a sprinkling of mounted bow-men. The reason was that in the countries to the south and west of the Danube and Rhine Rivers, there existed as yet no breeds of horse suitable for military purposes. Besides, most of Greece was hilly, not the sort of country where cavalry could excel. In Asia however, where there was an abundance of flat land, the horse-soldiers predominated.

tamed for riding and pack work, probably by reindeer herdsmen. Later they were broken for harnessing to chariots. Before 600 BC, all the 'horses' ridden or driven by ancient civilisations were in fact ponies!

This beautiful Arabian colt shows the fine quality inherited from the steeds of the Mohammaden horsemen.

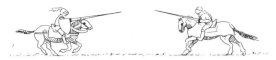

In London, the days of old are recalled by the ceremonial cavalry parade by the Queen's guard.

The cavalry are coming!

In the fifth century BC, when the Asiatic horsemen first came into contact with European foot soldiers, the idea of a combined army, with cavalry and infantry supporting one another, began to take root. Philip of Macedon, the great Greek king and general, founded the use of cavalry in the West. He created superb forces of horsemen, one cavalry-man to every six foot soldiers, and divided them into three sorts: the heavy armoured cavalry were for charging the enemy; the light cavalry (Hussars) acted as scouts and patrols; and the Dragoons were trained to fight on foot or on horseback. To defend his infantry against opposing cavalry, he massed the foot-soldiers into tight formations (phalanxes) armed with pikes 6 m long, to form an impenetrable hedge of steel. Philip's son, Alexander the Great, proved the effectiveness of this strategy in countless battles.

The Romans were rather slow in appreciating the value of cavalry, and when they eventually began to use horsemen in large numbers they made the serious mistake of separating them from the infantry. This error was the main cause of the decline of Rome's military power, for unsupported Roman cavalry were no match for the fierce barbarian horsemen who came riding in from the East, combining superb horsemanship with the added advantage of a highly-developed stirrup they had perfected, which meant they could mount their steed more easily, and gave them greater stability once on horseback.

At the end of the fourth century AD, cavalry became the main fighting force of

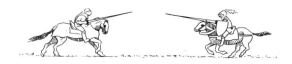

This fifteenth century war horse was as elegantly armoured as the knight who rode him.

European armies and remained so for over a thousand years. Between AD 500 and AD 1200 there were many well-equipped cavalry armies in the Middle East. In the West however, the key importance of the cavalry/infantry combination was forgotten. By the Middle Ages, Europe's preferred style of mounted fighting man was the knight, a self-contained 'armadillo' dependent on his heavy armour for safety and success, who wrongly assumed that he would always be opposed by a similarly iron-clad enemy. Heavy armour on a mounted man certainly gave him protection but it sacrificed his mobility, and the armour his horse now wore made matters even worse. By the mid-1300s some knights were so heavily armoured that, exhausted after repeated charges, their adversaries were able to roll them out of their saddles by grabbing their shoulders.

Haflinger ponies grazing on a Tyrollean meadow resemble the mounts of the Mongul horsemen.

Meanwhile the Mongols of the East, under the leadership of Genghis Khan, were showing what a disciplined, unarmoured cavalry could achieve. His men rode tough Mongolian ponies. Commanded in battle by means of signals from black or white flags during the day and coloured lanterns and whistling arrows at night, using smoke screens and fighting with bows and arrows to avoid close combat, they moved with impressive fluidity and flexibility – totally unlike their European counterparts. In the fifteenth century, Tamburlaine (Timur the lame), a chieftain from central Asia, repeated the empire-building success that Genghis Khan had achieved over 200 years before, but on horses that were bigger (cobs about 15.2 hands high) and of even better quality.

The fifteenth century saw the dawn of the age of gun-powder. As armour was not invulnerable to the bullet, it grew lighter, and the horse now carried a man armed with a hand cannon or arquebus.

When Cortes, the Spanish conquistador, invaded the Aztec kingdom on horseback in Mexico in 1519, his expedition almost failed; it was the horse that saved the day. The Aztecs had never before seen horses, and the animals tipped the balance in favour of the invaders, often by scaring the natives into fleeing. But for the horse the later history of South America would have taken a totally different course, and Spanish would not now be the language of countries from Mexico to Argentina.

As the centuries passed cavalry squadrons played major roles in the Napoleonic wars, the Boer War in South Africa and the First World War. A mere 50 years ago mounted soldiers were invaluable in the rough, mountainous terrain of Spain during the Civil War. In the Second World War however, the war-horse was increasingly replaced by a new kind of iron horse, the tank and the armoured car, though the horse's cousin, the mule, played a vital role in carrying heavy loads, including weapons and ammunition through many rugged places. In the Burmese jungle where allied troops fought the Japanese, mules were used to negotiate narrow, steep tracks. In order to prevent them alerting the enemy by uttering their characteristic braying sounds, army veterinary surgeons were called upon to operate on their larynxes (voice-boxes)

Right: *August 1917. Pack mules carry shells through the appalling mud of the battlefield.*

Below: *The American Indians had never seen a horse before.*

under anaesthetic in order to quieten their vocal cords – regrettable but essential surgery under the circumstances.

The veterinary service

Army horses have for centuries had army veterinary surgeons to look after their health problems in the same way that army doctors attend to the troops. Before qualified vets did this work, army farriers (blacksmiths) tended sick and wounded

In the First World War many horses wounded during battles were tended by the Army Veterinary Surgeons.

animals, and in the English army of the late sixteenth century military orders urged that there should always be 'a skillful Ferrar' who could judge soundness and lameness in the horses. In 1796 the British Army set up its Army Veterinary Service. Since then its vets have had not just horses as patients, but also camels, bullocks, cattle and donkeys. Most of the army vets' work then, as later, was in treating disease rather than battle wounds. In the Boer War one veterinary officer reported that of 4,170 cases of sickness in horses in his unit in two-and-a-half years of war, only 163 were due to bullet wounds and three to shell fire.

At the start of the First World War there were 53,000 horses in the British Army; there were six 250-'bed' (stall) veterinary hospitals, and 11 mobile veterinary units. As the war progressed however the number of horses rose to 450,000 with 18 2,000-'bed' veterinary hospitals! One curious consequence of the use of poison gas in that war was the issue of large gas masks to the horses. In the event, tens of thousands of horses were killed and wounded by gunshot wounds and bombs, but relatively few died from the effects of gas. In recognition of the Army Veterinary Corps' great work with horses during the war, King George V conferred the title 'Royal' upon it in 1918 and it became what it is known as today, the Royal Army Veterinary Corps.

In the Second World War, the RAVC accompanied pack animal units in Greece, Sicily, Italy, the Middle East, India and Burma. After this war they served again in Malaya, Kenya and Cyprus. As late as 1958 donkeys were employed to carry loads on the high mountain plateaux of Oman where the British Army was carrying out operations. One can imagine, in these days of guerilla warfare and civil unrest in Third World countries with difficult terrain, that horses, mules and donkeys, and their veterinarians, might well be called upon to serve with soldiers once more.

THE MODERN ARMY ANIMAL

It is 1962 in the battle-scarred area of Vietnam that the Americans call 'The Iron Triangle'. You, Ho-Chek, not long ago a peasant girl living in a village near Hanoi, sit cleaning your Kalashnikov rifle by the faint light of a lamp that is no more than a scrap of string in a tin cup full of old engine oil. Your chamber is a recess in the wall of a passageway barely big enough to hold three crouching people. The walls and roof are hard, dark soil and the air within is foul and humid. The passageway runs for 100 m east and west, and is connected by hidden trap doors to the main tunnel complex below. Down there, there are much bigger rooms, a small hospital, a kitchen, and several caches of explosives.

Sunlight, the green land, and the fresh, fragrant air are just 4 m above your head. But up there too is danger, destruction, and death. Napalm bombs, helicopter gunships and flame throwers brought by the armies of the United States, sear the once beautiful countryside with its tranquil paddy fields, vivid sunsets, lush jungle, water buffalo, and thatched hamlets. But still the Americans cannot believe, cannot know, with what effort and ingenuity you and your thousands of comrades in the Viet Cong have laboured to construct this vast underground labyrinth, this army camp in the earth, living like human moles. When they have sent men into the tunnels to investigate, they have encountered spiked traps, tethered poisonous snakes and trip-wired grenades; amongst all these dangers they have overlooked the concealed doorways and false walls.

By day you stay, fox-like, in the earth, but at night you emerge from the tunnels and go, clothed in black, shrouded by darkness, to attack and harass the enemy invader in his encampments.

'Ho-Chek.' Someone speaks your name softly. You raise the lamp and see the head of your section leader, Vam, emerging from the darkness in the western stretch of tunnel. He curls himself up against the wall of your chamber.

'We go soon?' you ask.

'Yes, Comrade.' He looks at his watch. 'In ten minutes. You know what you have to do?'

'Of course. Cut the wire exactly opposite the first parked helicopter. Wait for Comrade Ngi's diversion attack to begin in the north, and then go through with the explosives to position A.'

Vam nods.

'What though if the Americans do what they did last week?' you ask trying not to

A dog training unit of the US army in the Second World War.

33

One of the most popular working dogs for the armed services and police – the German shepherd dog.

sound too apprehensive. 'Everything went well until their guard patrol discovered Comrade Pak and his unit, even though they were well concealed.'

'Pak died honourably,' replies Vam. 'They all did. But what you say is true, the Americans can find us, using those . . . those devils. But I have the answer here.

Hanoi command came up with the idea.' He pulls a small bag out of his tunic and hands it to you. 'Here. Take these and rub them all over you before we go. That will put them off.'

You open the bag and look at the contents – several rotting cloves of garlic and a few blackened onions. The smell is pungent. A smile, a rare sight these days, begins to form on your lips. Of course! This should take care of those accursed Yankee war *dogs*!

During the Vietnam War the Viet Cong guerillas found that the trained dogs, *German shepherds* and *Dobermann pinschers* mainly, employed by the US Army to guard bases and accompany patrols, could be countered at least as far as their important sense of smell was concerned, by rubbing one's body with, and wearing bags containing, very pongy things.

An order issued by the Viet Cong Military Command reads: 'To make the dogs lose their sense of direction when they are chasing us, confuse their sense of smell with mixed odours. Garlic, onions, perfumes like eau-de-Cologne and overripe peppercorns will all make difficulties for them. When we camouflage ourselves, we should use these items by spreading them either on our bodies or over the vent holes of our underground hideouts. When in close combat, aromatic foods like fried fish and roasted meat can be thrown to the dog to put him off. You should also discard your sweating jacket or shirt to distract him . . .'.

Nowadays armed forces of many nations enlist trained dogs to perform a variety of duties. They can guard, track, carry messages, act as attackers and defenders. The military make use of their superb senses of smell and hearing as well as their speed, strength, intelligence . . . and their sharp teeth!

Selected breeding

The dog evolved as a versatile hunting carnivore, full of stamina and able to cope with a range of environments. The wild canid family from which the domestic dog is descended are masters of the long distance chase, wearing down their prey by sheer persistence, quite unlike the brilliant, ultra-fast, but essentially short-distance, wild cats. Domestication of the dog began around 10,000 years ago; much later selected breeding gave us the multitude of breeds that we know today. Man shaped the breeding of dogs to his own requirements, thereby obtaining general working dogs, dogs with more specialised working skills, and decorative dogs. He ended up with dachshunds for badger hunting, collies to herd sheep and miniature poodles just to look pretty.

One of the duties of a modern fighting dog is to guard airfields.

Dogs were probably used as guards soon after they were first domesticated by primitive man. Social animals, loving to be part of a family, canine or human, they are quick to raise the alarm by barking when a stranger intrudes. The dog became the first, and is today the most important, of man's military animals.

In 2100 BC, King Hammurabi of Babylon sent his warriors into battle accompanied by huge, fierce hounds. In Ancient Rome *mastiffs* in light armour, carrying spikes and cauldrons of flaming sulphur and resin on their backs, which would

dash among the enemy soldiers causing havoc. These canine 'tough guys' were formed into platoons and placed with the legionaries on the front rank. British 'broad-mouthed' dogs were prized by the Romans for their pugnacity in war and also for combat in the games held in the amphitheatres of the Empire. In the Middle Ages, armoured dogs, fully clad in metal, were used particularly against mounted knights. King Henry VIII sent

'Cave Canem!' I suppose mastiffs in the Roman armies must have understood commands in Latin.

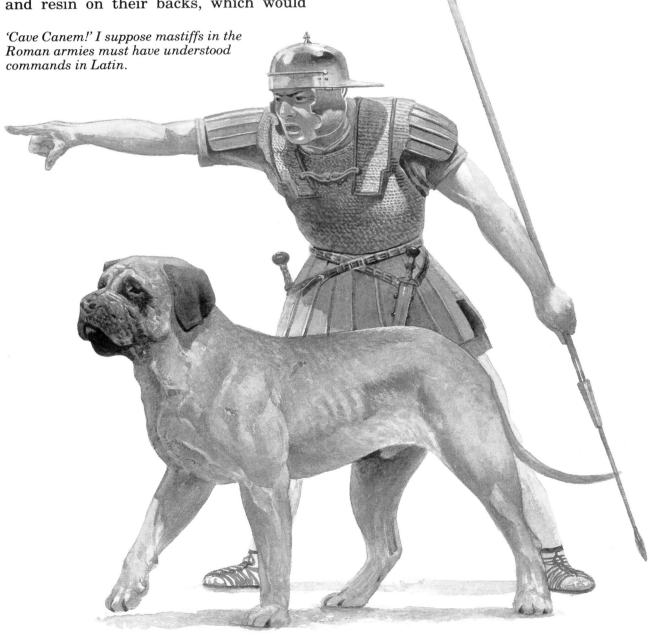

several hundred war dogs to Emperor Charles V of Spain to help him in his war with France, and they proved a great success. In the eighteenth century Frederick the Great used dogs both as sentries and as ammunition carriers when at war.

Training schools

At the beginning of the First World War, Britain had no official war dogs, though the Germans had over 6,000 ready and

This French army dog carried grenades to the frontline troops during the First World War.

waiting. This was only remedied in 1916 when the first British war dog training school was established. Dogs were used at first as messengers, as guards, to locate wounded men (German war dogs were credited with saving at least 4,000 soldiers), and to a lesser extent, on patrols. *Airedales* and *collies* were at first the two

The boxer made a good guard for army posts in the Middle East during the First World War.

most popular breeds for the army, but eventually the Alsatian (German shepherd), a versatile, strong and intelligent animal supplanted them. For tracking and mine detection work, *labradors* were to prove superb, and *boxers* were highly regarded as guards in Middle Eastern war zones.

In the Second World War dogs played a much bigger role than formerly, and sometimes in very unpleasant ways. They were trained by the Russians to carry out suicide missions against German tanks. They would run between the tracks of the vehicles with mines strapped to their backs. The mine would explode as soon as a vertical antennae attached to it touched the metal of the tank. I am glad to say that no-one trains dogs as 'living bombs' anymore!

In the British Army patrol dogs accompanied groups of soldiers on reconnaissance and, working silently, located by smell any hidden enemy. Then, like a gundog, they would freeze and 'point' in the manner of a setter or pointer. Mine-detecting dogs, again working by scent, could easily locate buried mines, either planted recently or long ago, at depths up to 30 cm. Dogs are better at this than most electronic sniffing devices! Some dogs were parachuted in with SAS units or the stretcher bearers of airborne divisions. These dogs were trained to search only for men lying in a prone, and therefore prob-

ably injured, position and to ignore all others. Such brave and clever dogs saved many allied soldiers' lives. Message-carrying dogs were trained to carry notes in a pouch on their collar between command posts and outposts or patrols.

Dogs continue to be trained and cared for by the British and other Armed Forces and have been on duty in Malaya, Kenya, Korea, Cyprus and, more recently, the Falklands and Northern Ireland. In Northern Ireland their abilities as guards and explosive-detectors have proved invaluable. The prestige and popularity of the fighting army dog has never been greater than at present. While army horses are nowadays only used for ceremonial purposes, the army dogs 'soldier on', and my colleagues the veterinarians of the RAVC and US Armed Forces have become specialists in canine medicine and surgery – 'horse-doctors' no longer.

The natural skills of a pointer accustomed to finding gamebirds, proved useful in the Second World War for locating injured soldiers.

Cry 'Havoc!' and let slip the dogs of war
Shakespeare *Julius Caesar* (Act III, Sc. i)

*I*magine. It is July 1950 in the north-eastern desert of Arabia, and you Salim bin Ahmed of the Bani Hajir tribe, crouch pressed up against the *camel*'s flank, your *abba* (cloak) pulled over your head. The animal is kneeling with its tailend turned to the howling wind. Stinging sand drives with the wind turning the air the colour of lentil broth, and you cannot see the rest of the herd that should be lying but a few metres off. By the beard of the Prophet, this storm is insufferable! The summer heat alone is bad enough, but the flying sand makes breathing almost impossible.

The sandstorm began about three hours ago as a small black cloud on the horizon that grew quickly and spread to claim the whole border between sky and desert.

Then it clawed its way up the heavens to blot out the sun. *Wallah!* Let it not be true, as the Kuwaiti bedou say, that such storms will last for three, seven or even 14 days! Your father, camped at the wells half a day's camel-ride away will be worried. This is the first time he has trusted you to take his camels to the grazing on your own. Still, all will be well, you have two skins full of water.

Another hour passes miserably and you reach under your *dish-dasha* (smock) for the bag of dates your mother gave you. The sand has even got to them and coated them in grit. Just then the unthinkable happens. Out of the swirling brown cloud

To me one of the most romantic scenes in the world; camels at home in the deep desert.

several dark shapes loom. Camels and riders! Who . . . ?

'*Al-guwa!*' a gruff voice calls the greeting. 'What have we here?' Six bedou riders carrying rifles move up to you.

'A young lad of the Bani Hajir far away from his mother, eh?' Raiders from the Ajman tribe to the north!

'I am Salim bin Ahmed' you shout above the storm, throwing a quick glance at your rifle in its cloth holster half-covered by the camel. No use, the raiders already have their guns pointing at you. One of the strangers taps your camel with his stick and it rises making a grumbling gurgle. He snatches its headrope.

'Well, Salim bin Ahmed, we are going to lift your camels. You should thank Allah we did not shoot you.'

Burning with anger, unable to do anything to save your family's camels from these arrogant robbers, you spit in the sand. 'My father and the Bani Hajir will

descend upon you like vultures on dead goats,' you say through gritted teeth. 'You will regret this day!'

The Ajmanis laugh behind the *kaffiyas* pulled across their faces against the sand. Their leader raises his rifle and fires one shot into the air. 'Brave words, my little gazelle, but it is your good fortune we take your camels and not your life.' He pulls on his camel's head-rope to turn it and the others do likewise.

'*Yaum-kum sa'id*' they shout as they disappear into the storm. It means literally 'Have a happy day!'. May the *djinns* (spirits) of the sandstorm whirl them away.

For thousands of years camels were ideal for military purposes in desert areas. The bedou nomads of Arabia used them until quite recently for raids like the one described above, and for more serious acts of warfare. Traditionally one of the great

'sports' of the bedou was raiding. Such forays rarely lead to much bloodshed and were conducted according to a gentlemanly rule book which insisted that women be unharmed and included a list of 'permitted' items, including goats, camels, carpets and coffee pots, which could be 'legitimately' snatched. A favourite raiding time was summer when camels graze far from the wells, and under the cover of sandstorms. Raiders sometimes travelled great distances of 250 miles or more to attack a target, and for such gruelling desert journeys the camel was their vehicle. In raids of up to 100 miles distance a mixture of camels and horses in equal numbers was usually employed.

A camel can carry heavy loads for long distances without feeding or drinking.

The ungainly-looking leg of the camel is perfect for desert travel.

The ship of the desert

The camel, familiarly called 'the ship of the desert', is well designed for a military role that only since the Second World War has been taken over fully by tracked mechanical vehicles, armoured cars and helicopters. Just look at a camel's capabilities! It carries concentrated rations in the form of special fat in a 'rucksack', the hump, on its back, enabling it to go for many days without food. Unlike most other mammals it can lose one-third of its body weight in the form of water without becoming ill. The blood stays thin to a point at which it would have thickened fatally in a dog or horse. Apart from its resistance to water loss, the camel saves every drop of the precious liquid that it can by not panting, and by concentrating its urine and by only passing small quantities, taking the waste products back into its body for conversion into food. Thus it conserves water and allows its body to 'dry out' to a degree that would prove rapidly fatal for a human being. Camels have been known to go for three weeks without water. When they are at last able

BUUURP! The camel is a frequent grumbler and gurgler.

to drink their fill, they can regain 30 per cent of their weight in just ten minutes.

Other design features of the camel which assist a desert lifestyle are an insulating coat of thick hair which keeps heat *out* during the day, and conserves body heat during the often freezing desert nights; round, flat feet, that are good for spreading the weight when walking on soft sand; long, lush eyelashes which keep sand out of the eyes when the lids are half-closed but still permit vision; and slot-like closeable nostrils, which also act as a protection against blowing sand.

The British Army used camels in many campaigns in the Middle East. Camels are in their prime at about nine years of age and the Army considered seven to 12 year olds as being suitable for military purposes. There are different breeds of camel with some better adapted to certain conditions than others. Those from the fertile Egyptian delta are not as able to withstand periods of drought and scarce

food as desert-bred animals. Breeds from the Central Asian steppes are small and shaggy with manes like lions; they work well in deep snow but cannot stand the desert heat. Indian camels survive heat and thirst well, as do the strong, compact and short-legged Ethiopian camels. Somalia camels are lightly built, can go for long periods without water, but aren't as strong as the Indian ones.

Stoicism and stamina

Good camels have amazing stamina. They can carry 120-220 kg for 32 km a day. After a battle near Basra, Iraq, in 1915, a messenger rode one 848 km in five and a half days to bring news to the Saudi king of a British victory over the Turks. The animals can travel for up to 160 km with rest halts every 32 km or so at a fast pace of 16 kmh. For short distances they can manage 21 kmh.

Camels are less liable to panic under gunfire than other animals and if made to kneel will remain so, quiet and contented. Some breeds such as the Somali, are rather nervous of strangers and are also

43

more jumpy at night. They bear pain with great fortitude and, unfortunately, will continue to work beyond a point of exhaustion at which other species would give up or collapse. They cannot jump across ditches – gaps in the ground over which they cannot stride constitute major obstacles; but they are strong swimmers and have been seen crossing the Nile even where the river is at its broadest and the current powerful.

The first Camel Corps to serve with the British Army was formed in 1884 in Egypt as part of a relief expedition going to Khartoum to rescue General Gordon. Later the Corps became a permanent part

The glamorous Camel Corps served efficiently in desert campaigns.

of the Army in Egypt and saw active service there, in Somalia, Palestine and other places.

One of the most romantic modern figures to be associated with battle camels was the Englishman T.E. Lawrence (Lawrence of Arabia) who fought with the Arabs against the Turks between 1915 and 1919. A brilliant leader of guerillas mounted both on camels and horses, he was particularly successful at wrecking Turkish trains, to such an extent that a large reward was offered for the capture of 'El Orens, destroyer of engines'!

> *Death is a black camel, which kneels at the gates of all.*
> Abd-El-Kader

These Toureg nomads carried out raids on their camels until fairly recently.

If you ever get the chance to ride a camel, perhaps when on holiday or at the zoo, take it. The animal's gait is quite different from that of a horse or pony and takes a little getting used to. I find it very exciting. The sight of Bedou nomads riding camels in the deep desert (they are still to be found in countries bordering the Arabian Gulf) is one of the most stirring and romantic things that I can recall. Bedou raiders of the Ajmani tribe would ride on a camel sitting *behind* the hump on a straw-stuffed mattress attached by ropes on the left and right, fixed to a girth in front of the hump. Other Bedou prefer to sit on the hump itself, a sheepskin saddle beneath them, with a pointed wooden pommel rising in front and another behind.